THOMSON
COURSE TECHNOLOGY

*NEW PERSPECTIVES*

MICRO
OFFICE

# Access 2003

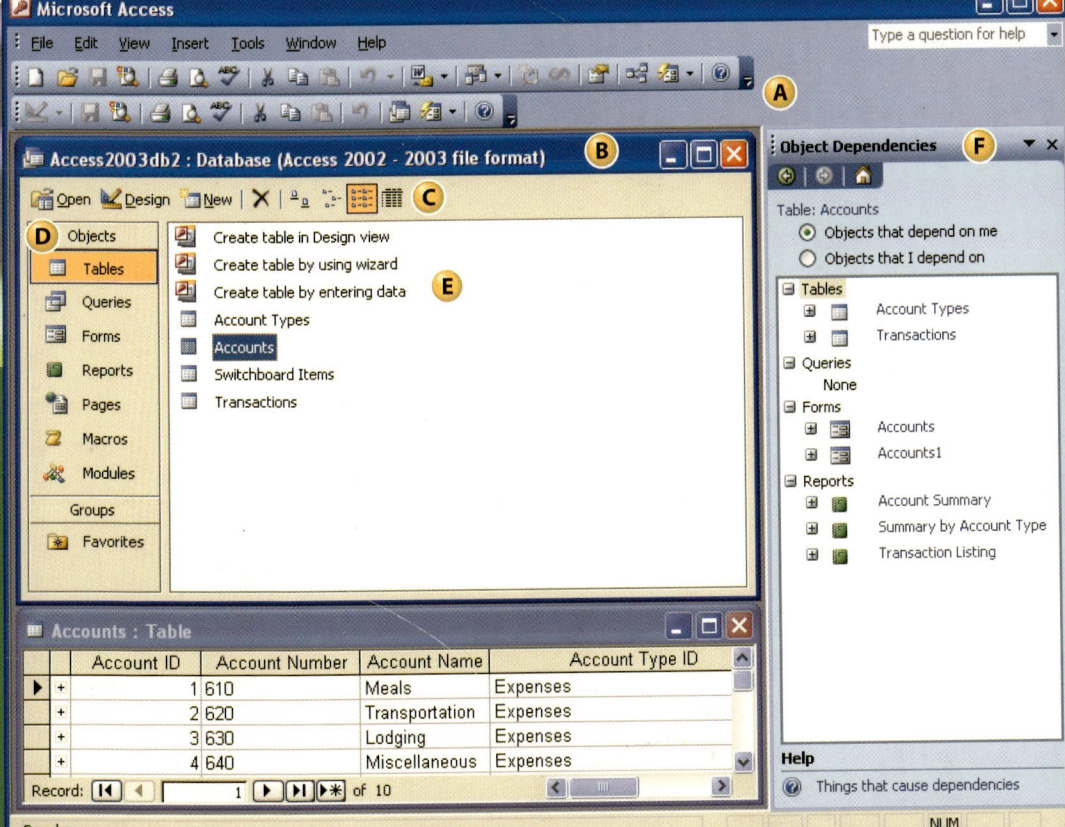

## Menu Quick Reference

Access menus
- File
- Edit
- View
- Query
- Insert
- Tools

Pages 2 and 3

## Basic Topics

Everyday activities
- Name database files and objects
- Set a primary key
- Add a record to a table datasheet
- Manually create a query
- Use the Report Wizard to create a report

Page 4

**(A) Toolbars**
Contain buttons and drop-down lists for performing common tasks, such as creating new objects 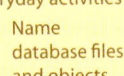, viewing object properties, displaying object relationships, and analyzing tables and database performance.

**(B) Database window**
Provides a command center for working with database objects. This window is displayed whenever you create or open an Access file.

**(C) Database window toolbar**
Contains buttons for common database tasks, such as opening, creating, and deleting objects.

**(D) Objects/Groups bar**
Displays all available object types and groups for a database. To display a list of all available objects of a particular type, click the appropriate button under Objects, such as  Tables or Forms. To display a list of all objects in a group, click the corresponding button under Groups.

**(E) Object list**
Lists all available objects of the selected type, along with shortcuts for creating new objects. When you double-click an object, it will open in the object's default view—for example, a table will open in Datasheet view. To switch to Design view, click  on the Datasheet toolbar.

**(F) Task pane**
Provides shortcuts for performing common tasks. To switch to a different task pane such as Help, New File, or Object Dependencies—click the down-arrow in the upper-right corner.

## Advanced Topics

Tables, queries, macros, and online integration
- Restrict data entry with input masks
- Create a table based on a query
- Improve performance through indexing
- Create a macro
- View object dependencies

Page 5

## Top Productivity Tips and Solutions

Useful time savers
- Create multiple primary keys
- Customize a form's tab order
- Convert a report to a Word document
- Optimize database performance

Page 6

ISBN-13: 978-0-619-26811-4
ISBN-10: 0-619-26811-5

# Menu Quick Reference

## File

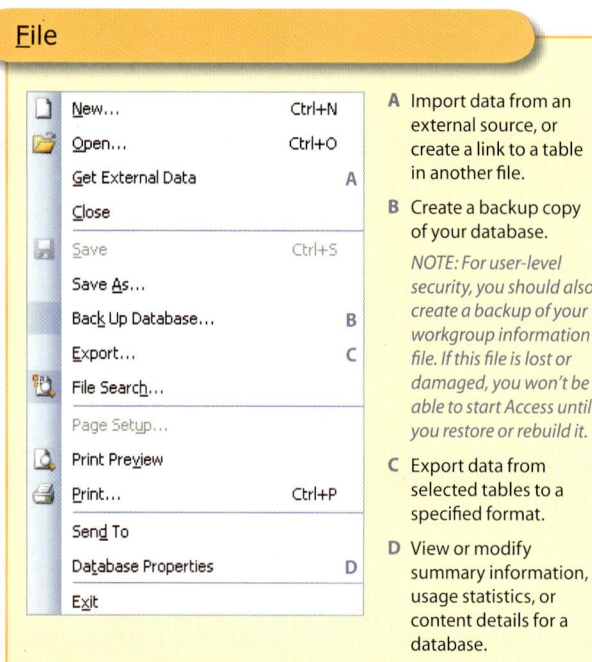

| | | |
|---|---|---|
| New... | Ctrl+N | |
| Open... | Ctrl+O | |
| Get External Data | | A |
| Close | | |
| Save | Ctrl+S | |
| Save As... | | |
| Back Up Database... | | B |
| Export... | | C |
| File Search... | | |
| Page Setup... | | |
| Print Preview | | |
| Print... | Ctrl+P | |
| Send To | | |
| Database Properties | | D |
| Exit | | |

**A** Import data from an external source, or create a link to a table in another file.

**B** Create a backup copy of your database.

*NOTE: For user-level security, you should also create a backup of your workgroup information file. If this file is lost or damaged, you won't be able to start Access until you restore or rebuild it.*

**C** Export data from selected tables to a specified format.

**D** View or modify summary information, usage statistics, or content details for a database.

## Edit

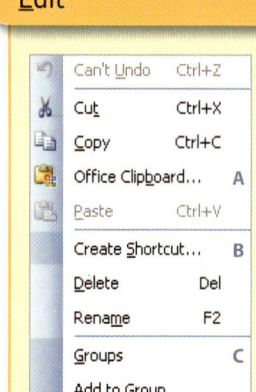

| | | |
|---|---|---|
| Can't Undo | Ctrl+Z | |
| Cut | Ctrl+X | |
| Copy | Ctrl+C | |
| Office Clipboard... | | A |
| Paste | Ctrl+V | |
| Create Shortcut... | | B |
| Delete | Del | |
| Rename | F2 | |
| Groups | | C |
| Add to Group | | |

**A** Use the Clipboard task pane to manage copied and cut items.

**B** Create a shortcut to a database object in another Access file. The target file can be stored locally, remotely on a network file server, or in a shared directory.

*NOTE: If you move the target file after creating the shortcut, delete the shortcut and create a new one. To delete a shortcut, select it and press* DELETE *. Remember, deleting a shortcut does not delete the object that the shortcut opens.*

**C** Create, rename, or delete a named group of database objects, or display frequently used forms and reports.

## View

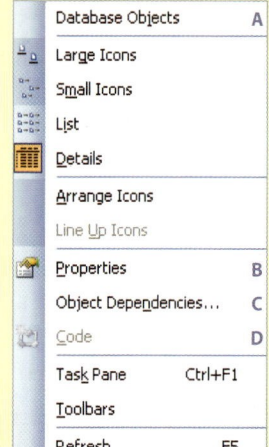

| | | |
|---|---|---|
| Database Objects | | A |
| Large Icons | | |
| Small Icons | | |
| List | | |
| Details | | |
| Arrange Icons | | |
| Line Up Icons | | |
| Properties | | B |
| Object Dependencies... | | C |
| Code | | D |
| Task Pane | Ctrl+F1 | |
| Toolbars | | |
| Refresh | F5 | |

**A** Display a list of all available objects of a particular type (queries, for example), along with shortcuts for creating new objects of the selected type.

**B** View or modify an object's properties. You can also enter a description for the object.

**C** Display the Object Dependencies task pane, which provides a list of all objects that use the selected object.

**D** Use Microsoft Visual Basic to write or edit procedures (macros) that dynamically create, delete, and modify data in the selected database object.

## View (Table Design view)

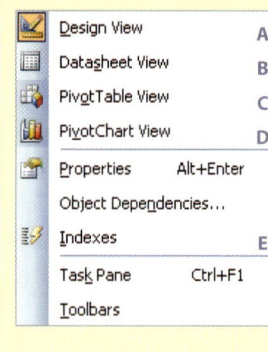

| | | |
|---|---|---|
| Design View | | A |
| Datasheet View | | B |
| PivotTable View | | C |
| PivotChart View | | D |
| Properties | Alt+Enter | |
| Object Dependencies... | | |
| Indexes | | E |
| Task Pane | Ctrl+F1 | |
| Toolbars | | |

**A** Display the selected table in Design view.

**B** Display data from a table, form, query, view, or stored procedure.

**C** Create a PivotTable view for the selected table or form. In this view you can add, move, or remove fields, and filter, sort, or group data.

**D** Create a PivotChart view (histogram) for the selected table or form.

**E** Create an index for the selected table.

## View (Query Design view)

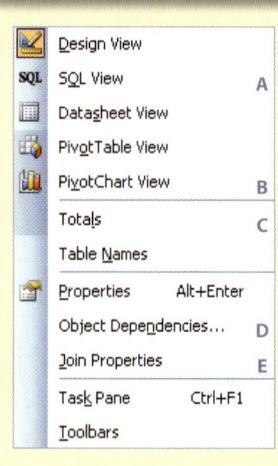

| | | |
|---|---|---|
| Design View | | |
| SQL View | | A |
| Datasheet View | | |
| PivotTable View | | |
| PivotChart View | | B |
| Totals | | C |
| Table Names | | |
| Properties | Alt+Enter | |
| Object Dependencies... | | D |
| Join Properties | | E |
| Task Pane | Ctrl+F1 | |
| Toolbars | | |

**A** View or edit the SQL code for the selected query.

**B** Create a PivotChart view (histogram) for the selected query.

**C** Calculate totals on all or selected records in a query.

**D** Display a list of objects that depend on the selected query.

**E** Create or modify a join query. You can combine records from two tables by creating a query that shows only the desired information.

## View (Form Design view)

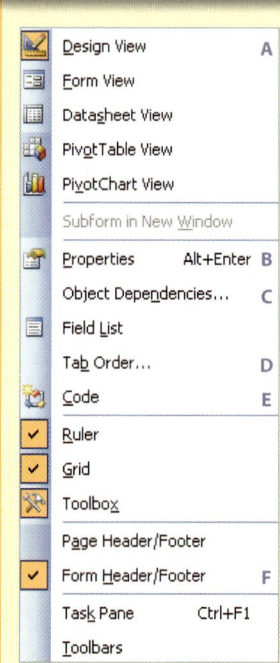

| | | |
|---|---|---|
| Design View | | A |
| Form View | | |
| Datasheet View | | |
| PivotTable View | | |
| PivotChart View | | |
| Subform in New Window | | |
| Properties | Alt+Enter | B |
| Object Dependencies... | | C |
| Field List | | |
| Tab Order... | | D |
| Code | | E |
| Ruler | | |
| Grid | | |
| Toolbox | | |
| Page Header/Footer | | |
| Form Header/Footer | | F |
| Task Pane | Ctrl+F1 | |
| Toolbars | | |

**A** Display the selected form in Design view.

**B** View or specify properties for the selected form.

**C** Display a list of objects that depend on the selected form.

**D** Customize the order in which form controls are activated when the user presses TAB . You can create a standardized order by clicking **Auto Order**.

*NOTE: In Design view, tabs are initially arranged in the order in which you create them.*

**E** Use Microsoft Visual Basic to write or edit procedures (macros) that dynamically create, delete, or modify data and the form.

**F** Specify a header or footer for the form.

# Advanced Topics

## Tables

### Create relationships between tables

1. On the Database toolbar, click the Relationships
2. On the Database toolbar, click the Show Table button to open the Show Table dialog box.
3. Select the desired tables, click **Add**, and click **Close**.
4. In the Relationships window, drag a field from the first table to a field in the second table. The Edit Relationships dialog box will appear.
5. Click **Join Type** to open the Join Properties dialog box. Then, select the desired option and click **OK**.
6. Check **Enforce Referential Integrity** and click **Create**.

### Restrict data entry with input masks

1. Open the desired table in Design view.
2. Select the field to which you want to apply an input mask.
3. Under Field Properties, on the General tab, place the insertion point in the Input Mask box.
4. Next to the Input Mask box, click the Build button to start the Input Mask Wizard.
5. Select the desired input mask and click **Finish**.

   | Input Mask: | Data Look: |
   | --- | --- |
   | Phone Number | (206) 555-1212 |
   | Social Security Number | 831-86-7180 |
   | Zip Code | 98052-6399 |
   | Extension | 63215 |
   | Password | ******* |
   | Long Time | 1:12:00 PM |

   *NOTE: If you want to create a custom input mask, click **Edit List**.*
6. Close the table. When prompted to save changes, click **Yes**.

### Create a table based on a query

1. Open the desired query in Design view.
2. Choose **Query**, **Make-Table Query**.
3. In the Table Name box, enter a name for the table that will be created.
4. Click **OK**.
5. On the Query Design toolbar, click the Run button to create the new table.

### Improve performance through indexing

1. Open the desired table in Design view.
2. Choose **View**, **Indexes** to open the Indexes window.
3. Under Index Name, select a blank cell.
4. Enter a name for the index and press ( TAB ).
5. Under Field Name, from the drop-down list, select the field to be indexed, and then press ( TAB ).
6. Under Sort Order, from the drop-down list, select the desired option— Ascending or Descending.

   | Index Name | Field Name | Sort Order |
   | --- | --- | --- |
   | LastName | LastName | Ascending |
   | PostalCode | PostalCode | Ascending |
   | PrimaryKey | EmployeeID | Ascending |
   | IndexName | HireDate | Ascending |
7. Close the Indexes window.

## Online integration

### Use the Page Wizard to save data in HTML format

1. In the Database window, under Objects, click **Pages**.
2. Double-click **Create data access page by using wizard**.
3. Select the desired table or query, select the desired fields, and click **Next**.
4. Add the desired grouping levels (if any) and click **Next**.
5. Set the desired sort order (if any) for each field and click **Next**.
6. Specify a page title, select **Open the page,** and click **Finish**.
7. Close the page, click **Yes**, and save the HTML file.

### [Enter] a SQL statement in a query

1. [In the Datab]ase window, under Objects, click **Queries**.
2. Double-click **Create query in Design view**.
3. Select the tables you want to include, click **Add**, and click **Close**.
4. Choose **View**, **SQL View**.
5. Enter the desired SQL statement.
6. Save the query.

## Macros

### Create a macro

1. In the Database window, under Objects, click **Macros**.
2. Click to open a blank Macro window.
3. Under Action, from the drop-down list, select the first action.
4. In the accompanying Comment field, enter a description for the specified action.
5. Enter the remaining actions and their descriptions.
6. Save the macro. To run it, click on the Macro Design toolbar.

## Queries

### Copy data between tables

1. Create a query that extracts the data you want to copy to another table. Then, open the query in Design view.
2. Choose **Query**, **Append Query** to open the Append dialog box.
3. From the Table Name list, select the table to which you want to append the extracted data, and then click **OK**.
4. Save and run the query.

## Editing

### Turn error checking on or off

1. Choose **Tools**, **Options**.
2. Activate the Error Checking tab.
3. Under Settings, check or clear **Enable error checking**.
4. Under Form/Report Design Rules, set the desired options.

   *NOTE: To change the color of the error indicator, use the provided drop-down list*

### View object dependencies

You can use a task pane to view dependency information for an open object or the selected object in the Database window. Here's what you do:

1. Choose **View**, **Object Dependencies** to display the Object Dependencies task pane. By default, this pane provides a list of all objects that use the selected object. This list will include all dependent tables, queries, forms, and reports.
2. Select **Objects that I depend on** to view a list of objects that are being used by the selected object.
3. To expand an object in the list, click the plus sign (+) next to the object's icon.

   *NOTE: By default, hidden objects will not be displayed in the Object Dependencies task pane. To make all hidden objects visible, choose **Tools**, **Options**, activate the View tab, and check **Hidden objects**.*

# Basic Topics

## Database creation

### Name database files and objects

Database and object names can have any combination of letters, numbers, special characters, and embedded spaces, with the following exceptions:

- Names cannot contain more than 64 characters and cannot start with a space.
- Names cannot include periods (.), exclamation points (!), accents (`), or brackets ([ ]).

*NOTE: It's a good idea to use underscores (_) between words instead of spaces.*

### Use the Database Wizard

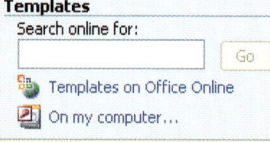

1. Choose **File**, **New**.
2. In the New File task pane, under Templates, click **On my computer**.
3. Activate the Databases tab, select the desired template, and click **OK**. The File New Database dialog box will appear.
4. Navigate to the desired storage location, enter a file name for the database, and click **Create**. The Database Wizard will start automatically.
5. Click **Next** and then follow the remaining steps of the wizard. You'll select fields, set styles for screen displays and reports, and specify a database title. When you're done, click **Finish**.

## Tables

### Create a new table

1. In the Database window, under Objects, click **Tables**.
2. Double-click **Create table in Design view**.
3. For each field you want to create, specify a field name, data type, and description. To apply additional control options, use the General tab (under Field Properties).
4. Choose **File**, **Save**, enter a name for the table, and click **OK**. If you have not defined a primary key, you will be prompted to do so.

### Set a primary key

1. Open the desired table in Design view.
2. Select the row that you want to define as a primary key.
3. Do one of the following:
    - Choose **Edit**, **Primary Key**.
    - On the Table Design toolbar, click 🔑.
    - Right-click the selected row and choose **Primary Key**.

    A key icon will appear next to the selected row to identify it as the primary key.

| | Field Name | Data Type | Description |
|---|---|---|---|
| 🔑 | Last Name | Text | Candidate's last name |
| | First Name | Text | Candidate's first name |

## Records

### Add a record to a table datasheet

1. In the Database window, double-click the desired table to open it in Datasheet view.
2. Select any cell in the table.
3. Choose **Insert**, **New Record** to create a new record at the bottom of the table.

    *NOTE: You can also use the New Record button ▶* on the Table Datasheet toolbar.*

## Queries

### Create a simple query

1. In the Database window, under Objects, click **Queries**.
2. Double-click **Create query by using wizard** to start the Simple Query Wizard.
3. Select the source table(s) for the query, add the desired fields, and click **Next**.

4. Enter a title for the query, select the desired option for viewing or modifying the query's design, and click **Finish**.

### Manually create a query

1. In the Database window, under Objects, click **Queries**.
2. Double-click **Create query in Design view**.
3. In the Show Table dialog box, on the Tables tab, select a table, click **Add**, and click **Close**.

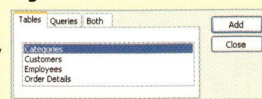

4. In the first cell of the Field row, use the drop-down list to select the desired field. Then, configure the desired parameters and criteria for your results.
5. Select and configure other fields as needed.
6. Choose **Query**, **Run** to test the query.
7. Save the query, or return to Design view to make changes.

## Forms and reports

### Use the Form Wizard to create a form

1. In the Database window, under Objects, click **Forms**.
2. Double-click **Create form by using wizard** to start the Form Wizard.
3. Select a source table and/or query, select the desired fields, and click **Next**.

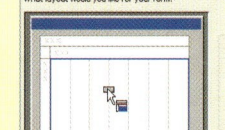

4. Select a form layout and click **Next**.
5. Select a form style and click **Next**.
6. Enter a title for the form, select the desired option for viewing or modifying the form's design, and click **Finish**.

### Locate data from forms

1. In the Database window, under Objects, click **Forms**.
2. Double-click the desired form to open it in Form view.
3. Place the insertion point in the field you want to search.
4. On the Form View toolbar, click the Find button 🔍.

5. On the Find tab, in the Find What box, enter the text or value you want to find.
6. Click **Find Next**.

### Use the Report Wizard to create a report

1. In the Database window, under Objects, click **Reports**.
2. Double-click **Create report by using wizard** to start the Report Wizard.
3. Select a source table, select the desired fields, and click **Next**.
4. Complete the remaining steps of the wizard. You'll select a layout and style for the report, and you'll specify a report title. When you're done, click **Finish**.

## Query

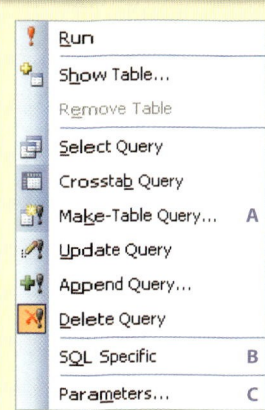

*NOTE: This menu is available only when you are working with a query in Design view.*

**A** Convert the current query to summarize data in a spreadsheet format.

**B** Create a data definition, pass-through, or union query to send commands directly to an ODBC database server.

**C** Create a query that prompts the user for information by establishing query parameters.

## Insert

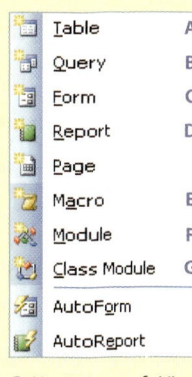

**A** Create a new table in the current Access database or project.

**B** Create a new query in the current Access database or project.

**C** Create a new form in the current Access database or project.

**D** Create a new report in the current Access database or project.

**E** Create a new macro in the current Access database or project.

**F** Create a new module in the current Access database or project.

**G** Use Microsoft Visual Basic to program or modify the code for a module. (You can use a class module to define a custom object.)

## Insert (Table Datasheet view)

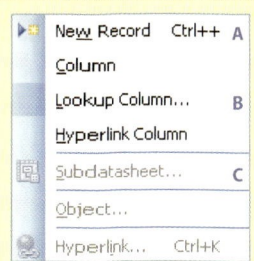

**A** Create a new record in the table.

**B** Create a lookup column that displays corresponding values from another table.

*NOTE: You can add multiple lookup columns to a table.*

**C** Create a datasheet that is nested within another datasheet and that contains data related or joined to the first datasheet.

## Insert (Query Datasheet view)

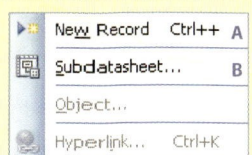

**A** Insert a new row in a query results datasheet.

**B** Insert a subdatasheet within a datasheet.

## Insert (Form Design view)

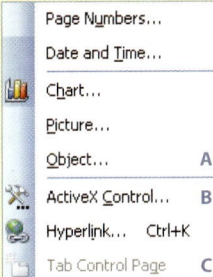

**A** Add an object—such as an image, a sound clip, or an Excel spreadsheet—to a form.

**B** Add an ActiveX control to a form.

*NOTE: Some ActiveX controls can pose a security risk, so it is recommended that you use controls only from trusted sources.*

**C** Add a new page tab to a tabbed form.

## Tools

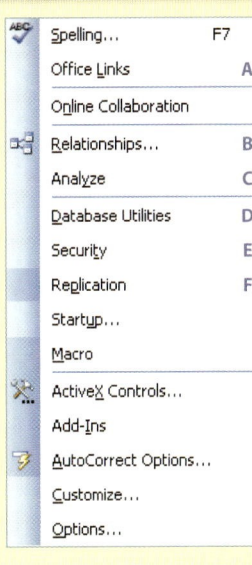

**A** Merge, analyze, or publish an Access object using Word or Excel.

**B** Display a diagram that shows the relationships between joined tables.

**C** Analyze tables and queries to enhance database performance.

**D** Convert, compact, back up, or repair a database.

**E** Specify a database password; set up accounts and permissions for users, groups, or the workgroup administrator; or encode/decode a database.

**F** Create or synchronize a database replica, resolve synchronization conflicts, or recover a replica set's Design Master.

# Top Productivity Tips and Solutions

### 1. Get more help with Access.

The following Web page contains many links to useful resources. Phone support is also available.

- **office.microsoft.com/assistance** (under BROWSE ASSISTANCE, click **Access 2003**)
- Free installation support: (425) 635-7056
- Paid technical support: (800) 936-5700

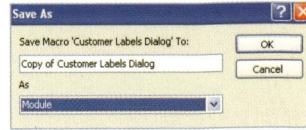

### 2. Go directly to Design view.

To avoid switching to Design view manually, you can open an object directly into Design view by holding `CTRL` and double-clicking the object.

### 3. Access additional shortcut menus.

When an object is open, you can right-click various items to display the associated shortcut menus. To access additional shortcut menus, right-click the gray areas of the open window.

### 4. Create multiple primary keys.

1. Open the desired table in Design view.
2. While holding `CTRL`, select the rows that you want to specify as primary keys.
3. On the Table Design toolbar, click the Primary Key button 🔑 to make each selected row a primary key in the table.

### 5. Customize a form's tab order.

1. Open the desired form in Design view.
2. Choose **View**, **Tab Order**.
3. Select the row you want to move, and then drag it to the desired position in the tab order. You can also select and drag multiple rows simultaneously.

   *NOTE: If you want Access to create a left-to-right and top-to-bottom tab order, click **Auto Order**.*

4. Click **OK**.

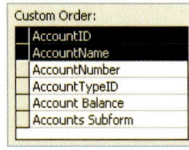

### 6. Convert a report to a Word document.

1. In the Database window, double-click the desired report.
2. Choose **Tools**, **Office Links**, **Publish It with Microsoft Office Word**. Word will start automatically and display the report as a document.
3. Save the document.

### 7. Search for text or values in a table.

1. Open the desired table in Datasheet view.
2. On the Table Datasheet toolbar, click the Find button 🔍 to open the Find and Replace dialog box.
3. On the Find tab, in the Find What box, enter the text or value you want to locate.
4. From the Look In list, select the name of the table.

5. Click **Find Next** to find the first occurrence of the specified text or value. Continue clicking this button until you locate the desired occurrence.

### 8. Force line breaks in Datasheet view.

To force a line break when entering text in a memo field, press `CTRL` + `↵ ENTER`.

### 9. Filter multiple columns simultaneously.

1. Open the desired table in Datasheet view.
2. Choose **Records**, **Filter**, **Advanced Filter/Sort**.
3. Select the fields by which you want to filter each column.
4. Specify the sort order and filter criteria.
5. Choose **Filter**, **Apply Filter/Sort**.

### 10. Save a macro as Visual Basic code.

1. In the Database window, under Objects, click **Macros**.
2. Select the desired macro.
3. Right-click the selected macro and choose **Save As**.
4. From the Save As list, select **Module**.
5. Click **OK**.

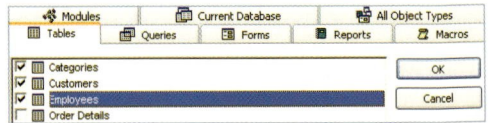

### 11. Optimize database performance.

1. Open the Database window.
2. Choose **Tools**, **Analyze**, **Performance** to start the Performance Analyzer.

3. Select the objects you want to analyze and click **OK**. The analyzer will present options for improving database performance.

### 12. Quickly import objects into a database.

To copy objects from one database to another, follow these easy steps:

1. In separate instances of Access, open the source and target databases.
2. Drag the object icon from the source database to the target database.

### 13. Return only the top few records in a query.

1. In the Database window, under Objects, click **Queries**.
2. Double-click **Create query in Design view**.
3. Select the desired tables, click **Add**, and click **Close**.
4. Choose **View**, **SQL View**.
5. In the Select Query window, after SELECT, type **TOP** followed by the desired number of records followed by a space and * (as shown in the example below).

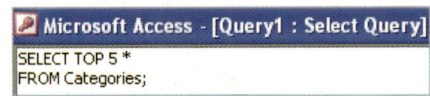

6. On the Query Design toolbar, click 🔴 to run the query, which will return the specified number of records.

### 14. Make macros run faster.

To turn off screen activity when running a macro, add th[is] line to the beginning of your macro code:

```
Application.Screenupdating = False
```